Healing in His Hands

A Devotional of Faith, Pain, and Purpose

A testimony of surviving breast cancer, reclaiming purpose, and rising stronger from every storm.

MELANIE E. LEWIS

Published by:
A Believer's Story Publishing
Houston, Texas
www.abelieversstory.live

ISBN: 979-8-9930450-1-6

Cover design by: Taminko Jones of CoolBird Publishing House
Edited by: CoolBird Publishing House

Printed in the United States of America

10 9 8 7 6 5 4 3 2 1

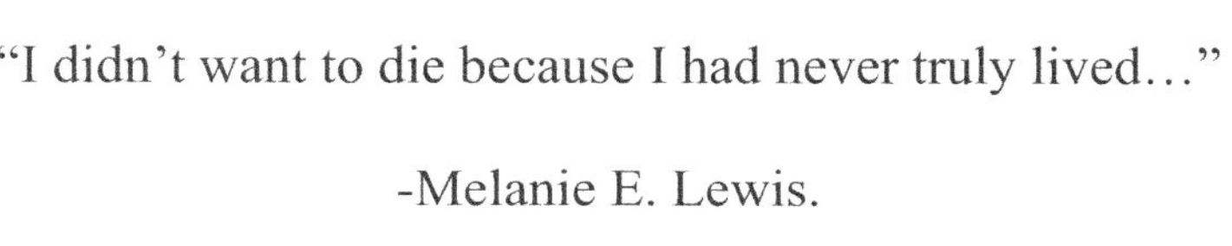

“I didn’t want to die because I had never truly lived…”

-Melanie E. Lewis.

Dedication

To my family-

Thank you for standing with me through every shadow and every sunrise. Your love, your prayers, your presence they carried me when I couldn't carry myself, thank you.

To every up and down, twist and turn, setback and setup that catapulted me into purpose… God used every moment, every scar, every silence, and every breakthrough for my good.

This is only the beginning.

Dear Reader-

I am opening my heart and history to share my story of how I survived the unthinkable; not just breast cancer, but emotional trauma, spiritual fatigue, and life-altering transformation.

From the quiet moments of surrender to the bold steps of faith, I will walk you through what it looks like to hold on to hope when everything else falls apart. This isn't just a story about pain it's my testimony of praise, perseverance, and purpose.

If you've ever questioned your strength, your faith, or your future… this book is for you because sometimes the storms don't stop but you learn that you were built to withstand them.

You are not alone. You are not forgotten. You are anchored through it all.

-Melanie E. Lewis

A – Assurance

God is With Me, Even in This
Overwhelm, Anxiety, Uncertainty

There are seasons when life feels like a storm with no calm in sight, just grief weighing on your chest, bills unpaid, health reports unclear, relationships broken and you may feel forgotten, but God's Word declares otherwise. In moments of overwhelming fear, the steady anchor of God's assurance is this: *You are not alone.*

In Isaiah 41:10 (KJV), God says,
"Fear thou not; for I am with thee: be not dismayed; for I am thy God:
I will strengthen thee; yea, I will help thee…"

This is not a weak promise. It's the voice of the Creator committing His presence, strength, and help to you. Assurance is the holy confidence that God is not only near but actively working all things for your good (Romans 8:28). Assurance doesn't mean your emotions disappear. It means your faith rises higher than fear. It means that even when the path is dark, you have a light. When life screams "uncertain," God whispers, *"I'm still here."*

Related Scriptures

- Isaiah 41:10 – "Fear thou not; for I am with thee…"
- Deuteronomy 31:8 – "The LORD himself goes before you and will be with you…"
- Hebrews 13:5 – "I will never leave thee, nor forsake thee."
- Psalm 23:4 – "Yea, though I walk through the valley… I will fear no evil: for thou art with me."

Personal Reflection

There was a time I felt completely unanchored. I was diagnosed with cancer, facing surgeries, radiation, and a future that seemed stripped from me, but even in the pit of physical pain and emotional collapse, I would hear that still, small voice say, *"You're not walking through this alone."* Assurance wasn't the absence of difficulty; it was the steady presence of God in the middle of it. That same assurance is available to you right now.

Prayer

Father, I thank You for Your presence. Even when I don't feel it, I trust that You're with me. When I'm overwhelmed, remind me of Your promises. Help me to walk by faith and not by sight. Fill my heart with Your peace and confidence. In Jesus' name, Amen.

Faith Declaration

I am never alone. God walks with me, leads me, and holds me steady through every storm. My confidence is anchored in Him.

Kingdom Key – Action of Faith

Take a sticky note or index card and write one of today's scriptures. Put it on your mirror, your desk, or inside your journal. Every time fear tries to rise, speak this scripture out loud and declare:

"God is with me. I am not afraid."

Journal Prompt

When have you felt overwhelmed or uncertain, yet saw God's hand guiding you through it? What did that season teach you about His presence?

____

____

____

____

____

____

____

____

____

____

____

____

____

____

____

B – Brokenness

When Life Breaks You, God Holds You
Pain, Grief, Shattered Dreams

Brokenness doesn't always show up in obvious ways. Sometimes it hides behind smiles, behind the ability to "keep going" even when your soul is barely standing. Whether your heart has been shattered by death, betrayal, illness, or disappointment God sees every crack, and He does not discard the broken.

The world treats brokenness as weakness, but in God's Kingdom, broken places become the birthplace of blessing.

"The LORD is close to the brokenhearted and saves
those who are crushed in spirit."
— *Psalm 34:18 (NIV)*

In your brokenness, you are not abandoned you are being held. You are not dismissed you are being drawn near. God's love does not recoil at your pain; it responds. It restores. It rebuilds.

In *2 Corinthians 4:7*, Paul reminds us that we are "jars of clay" fragile vessels that carry God's treasure. The cracks in our lives don't disqualify us from His purpose they allow His light to shine through.

Related Scriptures

- Psalm 34:18 – "The LORD is close to the brokenhearted…"
- Isaiah 61:1 – "He has sent me to bind up the brokenhearted…"
- 2 Corinthians 4:7 – "We have this treasure in jars of clay…"
- Psalm 147:3 – "He heals the brokenhearted and binds up their wounds."

Personal Reflection

There were days during my healing journey that I felt completely broken physically, emotionally, and spiritually. I questioned if I'd ever feel whole again. But in the stillness of those broken moments, I learned that healing isn't about having no scars it's about knowing who held you through the pain. I realized that Jesus was never repelled by brokenness. In fact, His ministry began with the brokenhearted. He embraced the wounded, the rejected, the weak. And He still does.

Prayer

Father, I give You the broken pieces of my heart every scar, every disappointment, every silent cry. I trust You to heal what I cannot fix. Use my brokenness for Your glory and help me to see Your beauty in every scar. In Jesus' name, Amen.

Faith Declaration

God is near me in my brokenness. I will not be defined by my wounds, but by His healing. Every shattered place in me is being restored by His grace.

Kingdom Key – Action of Faith

Take a few minutes to write a letter to God. Don't filter it. Tell Him how you feel your anger, confusion, sorrow, or grief. Then close the letter with a prayer of surrender: "Lord, I give this to You. I trust You with my brokenness."

Seal the letter in an envelope marked *"Healed by Grace."* Keep it in your Bible as a reminder that nothing is beyond God's power to restore.

Journal Prompt

What area of your life feels broken or incomplete? How do you believe God is working in that space even if you don't yet see the outcome?

____

____

____

____

____

____

____

____

____

____

____

____

____

____

C – Cancer & Courage

Faith in the Fight
Cancer, Health, Fear, Healing

No one is ever prepared to hear the word "cancer." It interrupts your life, shifts your identity, and floods your heart with fear. Suddenly, plans pause. Dreams dim. The future feels uncertain but while cancer may touch your body, it cannot cancel your purpose. While the diagnosis may try to shake your faith, it cannot silence the voice of God that says:

> "I shall not die, but live, and declare the works of the LORD."
> — *Psalm 118:17 (KJV)*

Courage in the face of cancer isn't about pretending you're not afraid. It's about showing up each day with a *mustard seed of faith*, declaring that your story isn't over because **God is not finished**.

You are not just a survivor. You are a warrior clothed in strength, sustained by grace, and infused with divine purpose.

Healing doesn't always look like a clean scan. Sometimes it's peace in the middle of treatment. Sometimes it's supernatural strength on a weak day. And sometimes, healing is eternal, whole, and victorious beyond this life. No matter what stage you're in diagnosis, treatment, remission, or supporting someone else know this: God sees you, He fights for you, and He walks with you through every step.

Related Scriptures

- Psalm 118:17 – "I shall not die, but live…"
- Isaiah 53:5 – "By His stripes we are healed."
- 2 Corinthians 12:9 – "My grace is sufficient for thee…"
- Joshua 1:9 – "Be strong and of good courage… for the Lord thy God is with thee."

Personal Reflection

When I was diagnosed with breast cancer, I was stunned. I wasn't ready. I didn't feel strong. I didn't feel "faith filled." But God didn't require perfection He required *presence.* I simply showed up, day after day, and let Him carry me. Each chemo visit. Each tear. Each prayer whispered when no one else was around God heard it all. And in time, I realized that healing wasn't just about my body it was about the healing of my soul, my confidence, my identity. The fight gave me fire and through that fire, courage was born.

Prayer

Heavenly Father, You know my diagnosis and every cell in my body. I ask for Your healing, Your strength, and Your peace. Replace fear with faith, and weakness with Your power. Let my story be a testimony of Your faithfulness. In Jesus' name, Amen.

Faith Declaration

Cancer is not my identity. I am courageous, covered, and called. My life will declare the works of the Lord.

Kingdom Key – Action of Faith

Today, speak directly to your body with the authority of God's Word. Say aloud: "I speak life, health, and healing over every system in my body. I am not a victim I am victorious through Christ Jesus."

If you're supporting someone else through cancer, write them a letter or text today reminding them they are not alone and they are deeply loved by both you and God.

Journal Prompt

What has this battle with cancer (or witnessing someone else's) revealed about your strength, faith, and the presence of God?

D – Deliverance

Freedom from What Tries to Hold You
Stress, Family Trauma, Emotional Strongholds

Deliverance isn't just about casting out demons or dramatic moments on an altar. It's about being set free from anything that keeps you bound fear, generational patterns, addiction, anxiety, bitterness, trauma, shame. God doesn't just save you to survive. He saves you to walk in freedom.

"It is for freedom that Christ has set us free."
— *Galatians 5:1 (NIV)*

The chains may be invisible, but the pain is real. Trauma from childhood, family dysfunction, cycles of abuse or abandonment these things don't just disappear. But they do break under the power of Jesus.

Deliverance happens when truth replaces lies, when healing replaces hiding, and when the Holy Spirit is invited to touch even the places we've shut off from others.

Don't let the enemy convince you that you'll always be "stuck." The blood of Jesus is strong enough to free you from every stronghold mental, emotional, spiritual, and physical.

Related Scriptures

- Galatians 5:1 – "It is for freedom that Christ has set us free…"
- Psalm 34:4 – "I sought the Lord, and He answered me; He delivered me from all my fears."
- Isaiah 61:1 – "To proclaim liberty to the captives…"
- John 8:36 – "If the Son therefore shall make you free, ye shall be free indeed."

Personal Reflection

There were times when I didn't even know I needed deliverance. I just thought it was "normal" to always feel on edge, to never trust people, to shut down emotionally, or carry the pain of my childhood into every relationship. But then I realized God didn't just want to heal my body…

He wanted to deliver my mind. He wanted to uproot fear, cancel generational curses, and reset the atmosphere around my life. Deliverance wasn't a one-time event it was a process. One "yes" at a time. And every yes made me freer than the day before.

Prayer

Lord, I give You permission to go into the deep places of my heart. Uproot what doesn't belong. Set me free from every lie I've believed, every fear I've carried, and every chain I didn't even know was holding me. Thank You that I don't have to stay bound I am free in You. Amen.

Faith Declaration

I am not a prisoner to my past. I am free, whole, and healed in Christ. Every stronghold in my life is broken by the blood of Jesus.

Kingdom Key – Action of Faith

Stand in front of a mirror today and speak directly to yourself:
"I am not who I was. I am free. I am healed. I am whole. Every chain is broken in Jesus' name."

Then write down any lies or labels you've carried. Tear that paper up. As you do, say out loud: "These no longer define me. I am who God says I am."

Journal Prompt

What are some hidden areas in your life emotional patterns, family issues, fears that may be keeping you from fully walking in freedom?

E – Endurance

Grace to Keep Going When You Want to Quit
Singleness, Waiting, Delays, Weariness

There's a part of every journey that feels the hardest not the beginning or the end, but the middle. The waiting season. The quiet place. The unanswered prayers. The ache of believing… and still not seeing. That's where endurance is born. Endurance is not about sprinting to the finish line. It's about trusting God when the finish line seems out of sight. It's the grace to *keep showing up* even when nothing looks like it's changing.

"But those who wait on the LORD shall renew their strength…"
— *Isaiah 40:31 (NKJV)*

In your singleness, in your silent seasons, in your "not yet" moments God is producing something eternal in you. Endurance teaches us how to lean. Not on our timeline, but on God's character. When the process feels slow, endurance reminds you that slow doesn't mean stuck. It means *sustained.* You're still here. Still moving. Still growing.

Endurance isn't easy but it's worth it. Because in the pressing, your faith is purified. In the waiting, your trust deepens. And through it all, God's strength becomes your own.

Related Scriptures

- Isaiah 40:31 – "They that wait upon the LORD shall renew their strength…"
- Romans 5:3–4 – "Suffering produces endurance… endurance produces character…"
- James 1:12 – "Blessed is the one who perseveres under trial…"
- Hebrews 12:1 – "Let us run with endurance the race that is set before us…"

Personal Reflection

There were seasons when I waited and waited and waited. For healing. For open doors. For answers. I watched others get married, get houses, get promotions, while I was still holding on to a promise that hadn't yet come to pass. It hurt. But I stayed. I trusted. I endured. And over time, I realized God wasn't just preparing *the blessing* He was preparing *me.* My capacity increased. My spirit matured. And what I thought was delay… was actually design.

Prayer

Lord, strengthen me to endure. Give me patience when I feel tired of waiting. Help me trust Your timing more than I trust my own expectations. Renew my faith when it starts to fade and give me fresh grace for the journey. In Jesus' name, Amen.

Faith Declaration

I have endurance. I am not forgotten. God is growing something good in me, even in the wait. I trust His timing.

Kingdom Key – Action of Faith

Write down a goal, promise, or prayer you've been waiting on. Next to it, write this: *"Even while I wait, God is working."*

Post this somewhere visible. Let it remind you that the middle of your story is just as meaningful as the ending. Celebrate your endurance because it's evidence that you haven't quit!

Journal Prompt

What have you been waiting for? What has that waiting season taught you about God and about yourself?

F – Forgiveness

Letting Go to Move Forward
Frustration, Family Conflict, Bitterness, Emotional Healing

Forgiveness is one of the hardest things we're asked to do especially when the wounds run deep. It feels unfair. It feels unnatural. But forgiveness isn't saying the offense was okay. It's saying: *"I'm not going to carry this anymore."* Forgiveness is freedom. Not for the other person but for *you.*

"Forgive us our debts, as we forgive our debtors."
— Matthew 6:12 (KJV)

Jesus knew the cost of betrayal. He was denied, abandoned, and crucified… and yet His words on the cross were: *"Father, forgive them."*

When we choose forgiveness, we're not excusing the behavior we're releasing the burden. Because bitterness is a prison with no door. It keeps us replaying the past while missing the beauty of the present. Forgiveness does not mean reconciliation is always possible. It means *you* are no longer hostage to the pain. And every time you forgive, you become more like Christ.

Related Scriptures

- Matthew 6:12 – "Forgive us our debts, as we forgive our debtors."
- Ephesians 4:32 – "Be kind to one another, tenderhearted, forgiving one another…"
- Colossians 3:13 – "Forgive as the Lord forgave you."
- Luke 23:34 – "Father, forgive them…"

Personal Reflection

There were people who hurt me and never apologized. People I trusted who turned their backs on me. For a long time, I thought forgiving them meant I had to pretend it never happened. But I learned something powerful: *forgiveness is not forgetting it's freeing.* It was when I released their names from my anger that God released *me* from the heaviness in my heart. Forgiveness changed me. It didn't rewrite the past, but it opened my future.

Prayer

God, I bring every offense, every wound, every name before You. I release the bitterness I've held onto. Help me to forgive like You forgive fully, freely, and with love. Heal my heart as I let go. In Jesus' name, Amen.

Faith Declaration

I choose to forgive. I release the hurt and the offender. I walk in freedom, healing, and peace through Christ.

Kingdom Key – Action of Faith

Take a blank sheet of paper and write down the names of people who have hurt or betrayed you. Once finished, pray over each name, saying: "God, I forgive them. I release them into Your hands."

Then rip the paper up. Don't throw it away in anger throw it away as a prophetic act of release. You are no longer bound. You are free.

Journal Prompt

Who do you need to forgive? What is holding you back from letting go? How do you think your life would change if you released the weight?

G – Grace

God's Love Covers What You Can't Fix
Grief, Parenting, Weakness, Acceptance

If mercy is God *not giving* us what we deserve, grace is Him *giving* us what we don't deserve: strength, favor, help, covering, love… especially when we feel unworthy.

- Grace says, *"I see your failure and still choose you."*
- Grace says, *"I know you're tired, and I'll carry you."*
- Grace says, *"You're not strong enough? That's okay My power is made perfect in weakness."*

"My grace is sufficient for thee: for my strength is made perfect in weakness."
— 2 Corinthians 12:9 (KJV)

We often feel pressure to have it all together especially as parents, caregivers, leaders, or just functioning adults. But God never asked for perfection. He asked for surrender.

- When you're grieving and trying to hold your family together… Grace holds you.
- When you're a single parent trying to be everything for everyone… Grace strengthens you.
- When your body is weak, your heart is heavy, and your hope feels fragile…

Grace surrounds you. You don't earn it. You don't work for it. You just receive it.

Related Scriptures

- 2 Corinthians 12:9 – "My grace is sufficient for thee…"
- Ephesians 2:8 – "For by grace are ye saved through faith…"
- Hebrews 4:16 – "Let us come boldly unto the throne of grace…"
- Romans 5:20 – "Where sin abounded, grace did much more abound."

Personal Reflection

There were days I didn't feel worthy to be called strong. I was in pain, overwhelmed, grieving, and barely making it. I missed appointments. Snapped at people. Cried without reason. And yet God met me with kindness instead of condemnation. That's grace.

It didn't erase my reality it embraced me in it. It reminded me that God isn't counting my failures. He's counting every time I get back up and trust Him again.

Prayer

Father, thank You for grace that covers, lifts, and restores. I receive Your help in my weakness. I release the pressure to be perfect and embrace the truth that Your grace is enough for me. Teach me to extend that same grace to others and to myself. In Jesus' name, Amen.

Faith Declaration

God's grace is covering me, carrying me, and keeping me. I am not alone, and I don't have to be perfect to be chosen. His strength is working through me.

Kingdom Key – Action of Faith

Choose one area where you've been hard on yourself lately your parenting, your body, your finances, your emotions. Write a note of grace to yourself, starting with: "I may not be perfect, but by God's grace, I am growing…"

Post it where you'll see it often. Let grace be your new standard.

Journal Prompt

Where in your life do you feel like you're not "enough"? How would your mindset shift if you believed that God's grace was more than enough for you in that very area?

____

____

____

____

____

____

____

____

____

____

____

____

____

____

H – Healing

God Heals More Than Just the Body
Sickness, Emotional Pain, Health, Trauma

Healing is more than the absence of illness. It's the restoration of wholeness body, mind, and soul. Sometimes, God heals instantly. Sometimes, He heals over time. And sometimes, He heals through tears, therapy, treatment, or the quiet surrender of trust.

Healing isn't always visible. You can be physically well and still broken inside. Or you can be sick in body but thriving in spirit. That's why the healing Jesus offers is deeper it touches the root.

"He heals the brokenhearted and binds up their wounds."
— *Psalm 147:3 (NIV)*

Whether you're battling disease, depression, trauma, or invisible scars God sees it all. And He promises not just to comfort you in the pain, but to restore you through it. You are not your diagnosis. You are not your past. You are not the labels spoken over you. God is the God of complete restoration. And if healing hasn't come in the way you expected, trust that it's still in progress.

Related Scriptures

- Psalm 147:3 – "He heals the brokenhearted..."
- Isaiah 53:5 – "By His stripes we are healed."
- Jeremiah 30:17 – "I will restore you to health..."
- 3 John 1:2 – "That you may prosper and be in health, even as your soul prospers."

Personal Reflection

When I was in treatment, there were days my body screamed for relief. But the deeper battle was in my soul fighting discouragement, fatigue, and fear. What surprised me most was how God didn't just touch my body He held my spirit. Healing began the day I stopped striving and started surrendering.

It was in worship, in rest, in vulnerability with God that I began to feel whole again. Healing became more than a goal it became a journey I walked hand-in-hand with the Healer.

Prayer

Jehovah Rapha, my Healer I lift every wound to You. Heal my body, heal my heart, heal my memories. Go to the places I've hidden and speak life again. I trust You to restore everything I thought was broken beyond repair. In Jesus' name, Amen.

Faith Declaration

I am being healed day by day, layer by layer. God is restoring what I thought was lost, and my healing will be a testimony of His power and love.

Kingdom Key – Action of Faith

Write down the name of one area where you're believing God for healing (e.g., "grief," "my lungs," "my heart," "my marriage"). Tape it somewhere you'll see daily. Every time you pass it, lay your hand on it and say: "Healing belongs to me. By His stripes, I am healed."

Begin to *thank God in advance* for the restoration that is already unfolding even if you can't see it yet.

Journal Prompt

What part of your life needs healing right now physically, emotionally, spiritually? How has God already begun the work of restoration?

I – Identity in Christ

You Are Who God Says You Are
Singleness, Loneliness, Worth, Confidence

When life strips you of titles spouse, employee, mother, healthy, needed it's easy to wonder: *Who am I now?* The world tells us our identity is in what we do or who we're with. But God's Word declares that your true identity is *not in your status, your mistakes, or your pain.* It is in Christ.

"Therefore, if anyone is in Christ, he is a new creation…"
— 2 Corinthians 5:17 (NKJV)

Your identity is not broken, hidden, or missing. It's eternal, sealed, and secure in Jesus. You are chosen. You are beloved. You are redeemed. And you are not alone.

In seasons of singleness or grief, when companionship is lacking or silence feels heavy, let this truth anchor your soul: Your value isn't diminished by your relationship status or the number of people who check in. God knows your name. And that's enough.

Related Scriptures

- 2 Corinthians 5:17 – "If anyone is in Christ… new creation."
- Ephesians 2:10 – "We are His workmanship…"
- 1 Peter 2:9 – "You are a chosen generation…"
- Romans 8:16 – "We are children of God."

Personal Reflection

There was a season where I felt invisible. The invitations stopped. The phone went quiet. The enemy whispered, "You're not needed anymore." But God reminded me I was never created to find identity in people. My worth isn't measured by attention, but by adoption. He called me His. And that was the beginning of true confidence.

Prayer

Father, remind me who I am when I forget. Show me how You see me worthy, loved, and chosen. Let my identity be rooted in You and not in what I've lost. Silence every lie that says I'm not enough. I am Yours. In Jesus' name, Amen.

Faith Declaration

I am not defined by my status I am defined by my Savior. I am who God says I am loved, chosen, whole, and complete in Christ.

Kingdom Key – Action of Faith

Write this on a card or mirror where you'll see it every day:

- My name is not 'Not Enough.'
- My name is not 'Alone.'
- My name is *Beloved Child of God.*"

When the enemy tries to rename you with words like forgotten, unworthy, or failure speak your real name out loud: *"I am His."*

Journal Prompt

Have you ever found your identity in a title or relationship that changed or ended? How did it impact you, and what truth is God revealing to you now?

J – Joy

Choosing Joy in the Midst of Sorrow
Depression, Isolation, Loss, Weariness

Joy is not the same as happiness. Happiness depends on circumstances joy depends on Christ. It is possible to be crying and still have joy. To be grieving and still have joy. To be in the valley and still declare, *"God is good."* Joy is a *fruit of the Spirit*, not a product of everything going right.

"The joy of the Lord is your strength."
— *Nehemiah 8:10 (KJV)*

When sorrow visits your doorstep or depression sits in your chest like an uninvited guest, joy doesn't mean pretending everything's fine. It means remembering that everything's *not finished*. The enemy wants to steal your joy because he knows it's your strength. But the Lord gives you joy not as a fragile feeling but as a firm foundation.

You can walk through loss and still experience moments of light, laughter, and peace. That's joy God's supernatural reminder that sorrow will not have the final word.

Related Scriptures

- Nehemiah 8:10 – "The joy of the Lord is your strength."
- Psalm 30:5 – "Weeping may endure for a night, but joy cometh in the morning."
- John 16:22 – "Your joy no man taketh from you."
- Romans 15:13 – "May the God of hope fill you with all joy and peace…"

Personal Reflection

I remember trying to smile through tears, to show up when my heart wanted to stay in bed. Grief and joy felt like they didn't belong in the same room until I realized that *joy is not the absence of pain it's the presence of God* in the pain.

The moment I allowed God to hold my sorrow, joy began to slowly reenter my heart. It came in the form of laughter I didn't expect. A quiet peace. A beautiful sunrise. The strength to try again.

Prayer

God, I thank You that joy is not something I have to earn. It's a gift. Fill me with Your joy, even while I'm hurting. Remind me that this pain is not permanent and that You are writing beauty into my story. In Jesus' name, Amen.

Faith Declaration

I will not let sorrow steal my song. The joy of the Lord is my strength, and His joy lives in me no matter what I feel or face.

Kingdom Key – Action of Faith

Today, choose one simple thing that brings you joy—music, nature, painting, laughter, cooking. Do it on purpose. Let yourself enjoy without guilt. Then, thank God aloud: "This joy is from You. And it is my strength."

Don't wait for your situation to change to embrace joy. Sometimes, joy *is* the change.

Journal Prompt

When was the last time you truly felt joy? What would it look like to invite God into your sorrow and ask Him to restore your joy?

K – Kingdom Focus

Living with Eternity in Mind
Vision, Purpose, Perspective, Surrender

It's easy to get caught in the cycle of surviving bills, health, heartbreak, disappointments. Life demands so much of us; it's tempting to live with tunnel vision. But God invites us to something higher: a Kingdom perspective.

> "But seek ye first the kingdom of God, and his righteousness;
> and all these things shall be added unto you."
> — *Matthew 6:33 (KJV)*

Kingdom focus doesn't ignore our reality it reorders our priorities. It reminds us that we weren't created just to make it through the day. We were created to walk in purpose, impact others, and bring heaven to earth.

This world is not our home. And when you live with that awareness, it changes how you respond to pain, delay, betrayal even cancer, grief, and loss. You realize: *"If it didn't come from God, it doesn't get to define me."*

A Kingdom mindset is not passive it's powerful. It means we don't just react to what happens… we align ourselves with what God is doing.

Related Scriptures

- Matthew 6:33 – "Seek first the Kingdom of God…"
- Colossians 3:2 – "Set your mind on things above, not on earthly things."
- Romans 14:17 – "The kingdom of God is not meat and drink; but righteousness, peace, and joy in the Holy Ghost."
- Philippians 3:20 – "Our citizenship is in heaven…"

Personal Reflection

When I shifted my focus from survival to *assignment,* everything changed. I no longer saw cancer as punishment, but as part of a testimony. I saw loneliness as preparation. I saw delay as divine setup. Kingdom focus taught me to stop asking "Why me?" and start asking, "Lord, how can You use me *in this*?"

Prayer

Father, align my mind with Your Kingdom. Help me to see beyond the temporary and live with eternal vision. Take the distractions that consume me and restore my focus to what truly matters Your purpose, Your people, and Your presence. In Jesus' name, Amen.

Faith Declaration

I live with Kingdom focus. My mind is set on things above, and my life reflects God's eternal plan. I will not be swayed by the temporary I am anchored in truth and purpose.

Kingdom Key – Action of Faith

Today, write down one Kingdom-centered goal something that serves others, advances God's work, or builds lasting impact. Pray over it. Then ask God to show you the *first step* toward making that vision a reality. Obedience is the gateway to Kingdom fulfillment.

Declare this out loud: "I am not just living to survive. I'm living to build God's Kingdom. My life has eternal impact."

Journal Prompt

What distractions have pulled your focus lately? How can you begin to live with more intentional, Kingdom-aligned purpose?

____

____

____

____

____

____

____

____

____

____

____

____

____

____

____

L – Loneliness & Love

You Are Never Truly Alone
Loneliness, Widowhood, Isolation, Abandonment

Loneliness is not just about being alone it's about *feeling* unseen, forgotten, or unworthy of connection. You can be in a room full of people and still feel completely invisible. But God sees what others overlook. And more than that, He is present.

"The Lord is close to the brokenhearted…" — *Psalm 34:18 (NIV)*
"I will never leave thee, nor forsake thee." — *Hebrews 13:5 (KJV)*

There is no void too wide, no silence too deep, that His love cannot reach. Maybe you're walking through widowhood and sleeping in a bed that feels too big now. Maybe you're single and wondering if your love story was skipped.

Maybe family and friends don't understand the ache you carry. God does. and He doesn't just *visit* you in your loneliness He *dwells* with you. And His love is not second-best. It's not a placeholder. It's the truest love you'll ever know.

Related Scriptures

- Psalm 34:18 – "The Lord is close to the brokenhearted…"
- Hebrews 13:5 – "I will never leave thee, nor forsake thee."
- Isaiah 49:15–16 – "I have engraved you on the palms of my hands…"
- Romans 8:38–39 – "Nothing can separate us from the love of God…"

Personal Reflection

There were nights when I felt like no one understood what I was going through. I felt invisible, even surrounded by people. But then I realized God wasn't just beside me... He was inside every moment, every tear, every sigh.

He reminded me: "Even if no one calls, I'm still speaking. Even if no one sees you, I've never taken My eyes off you." That love healed me. It filled places no human could reach.

Prayer

Father, I give You the empty spaces. The quiet nights. The ache of being misunderstood. Thank You for loving me perfectly. Wrap me in Your presence and remind me daily that I am never alone. In Jesus' name, Amen.

Faith Declaration

Even in silence, I am not abandoned. I am seen, known, and deeply loved by God. His presence is my constant companion.

Kingdom Key – Action of Faith

Write a love letter from God to you. Let it start with, *"My beloved child..."* and fill it with truths from scripture:

- "I have loved you with an everlasting love." (Jeremiah 31:3)
- "You are mine." (Isaiah 43:1)
- "You are never alone." (Matthew 28:20)

Post it somewhere visible. Every time you feel isolated, read His words again and remember: *You are His favorite kind of company.*

Journal Prompt

What does your loneliness look like right now? What is God showing you about His love in this season of solitude?

M – Mercy

God Doesn't Give Me What I Deserve He Gives Me Love
Family Struggles, Mistakes, Guilt, Redemption

Mercy is God's way of saying, *"I see your flaws, but I choose to love you anyway."* It's when He looks at our past, our choices, our pain and chooses compassion over condemnation. Mercy meets us not when we've "gotten it together," but when we're most desperate for grace.

"It is of the Lord's mercies that we are not consumed, because his compassions fail not. They are new every morning…"
— *Lamentations 3:22–23 (KJV)*

If you've ever said something you wish you could take back, if you've ever made a decision that hurt someone you love, if you've ever parented from a place of pain instead of peace you've probably wrestled with guilt. But here's the truth: God's mercy is bigger than your mistake.

In family relationships, mercy is what keeps the door open. It's what allows healing to enter instead of resentment. Mercy makes room for people to grow, and it reminds you that *you, too, are growing.*

Related Scriptures

- Lamentations 3:22–23 – "His mercies… are new every morning."
- Psalm 103:10 – "He has not dealt with us according to our sins…"
- James 2:13 – "Mercy triumphs over judgment."
- Luke 6:36 – "Be ye therefore merciful, as your Father also is merciful."

Personal Reflection

There have been moments I've lost my patience with family. Times I didn't extend the love I should have. I carried that guilt longer than I needed to until I remembered that mercy isn't just something *I give.* It's something *I receive.*

I learned to forgive others by first allowing God to forgive me. And I found peace not in being perfect, but in knowing that His mercy never runs out.

Prayer

Lord, thank You for Your mercy. I don't always get it right, but You love me anyway. Help me to extend the same mercy to others especially in my family. Heal the places where guilt or judgment have taken root, and let compassion grow instead. In Jesus' name, Amen.

Faith Declaration

God's mercy is new for me today. I release guilt and receive grace. I choose mercy over judgment, for myself and for others.

Kingdom Key – Action of Faith

Write down one area where you've been hard on yourself. Underneath it, write this: "God's mercy covers this."

Now write down the name of someone who may need mercy from *you*. Reach out with a kind message, a prayer, or a moment of patience. Let mercy do what only it can do: heal and restore.

Journal Prompt

Where in your life have you experienced God's mercy the most? Are there people you've struggled to show mercy to? Why?

N – Newness

God Makes All Things New Including You
Fresh Starts, Renewal, Transformation, Hope

We've all made decisions we regret. Lived through seasons we'd rather forget. Faced mornings where the weight of yesterday felt unbearable. But here's the promise of God: You are not stuck. You are not too far gone. You are not too broken.

"Therefore, if any man be in Christ, he is a new creature: old things are passed away; behold, all things are become new."
— 2 Corinthians 5:17 (KJV)

God is not intimidated by your past. He doesn't just patch you up He makes you new. Newness means you get to grow. You get to begin again. Even in the middle of your story, God can flip the script and give you a fresh page. His mercy is your reset button. His grace is your clean slate. You may still feel the sting of what was, but don't let it rob you of what can be. In Christ, your next chapter is already being written and it's drenched in purpose.

Related Scriptures

- 2 Corinthians 5:17 – "If any man be in Christ, he is a new creature…"
- Isaiah 43:18–19 – "Behold, I will do a new thing…"
- Lamentations 3:22–23 – "New every morning is Your mercy…"
- Ezekiel 36:26 – "A new heart also will I give you…"

Personal Reflection

When I came out of treatment and into a new chapter of life, I didn't feel "new." I still saw scars. I still carried memories. But as I looked deeper, I realized the newness wasn't just in my health, it was in my *hope*. God had done something internal. I had new eyes to see the future. A new voice to tell my story. A new walk, with more purpose in each step. Newness isn't always dramatic it's often quiet, steady, and sacred.

Prayer

Lord, thank You for making me new. I release the old mindsets, shame, and burdens that have kept me bound. Breathe fresh life into my spirit. Give me new vision, new strength, and a new beginning. In Jesus' name, Amen.

Faith Declaration

I am not who I used to be. I am new in Christ. Every day is a fresh start, and my life is moving forward in healing, purpose, and joy.

Kingdom Key – Action of Faith

Today, do something symbolic to represent your new beginning:

- Buy a new journal.
- Rearrange a room.
- Go for a walk in a new place.
- Speak a new declaration over yourself.

Say out loud: "God is doing something new in me. I embrace it with faith and expectation."

Journal Prompt

What "old things" are you ready to let go of today? What would it mean to fully step into the newness God is offering?

____

____

____

____

____

____

____

____

____

____

____

____

____

____

____

O – Overwhelmed

When Life Feels Like Too Much, God is Still Enough
Burnout, Mental Load, Emotional Fatigue, Surrender

Have you ever had days where the simple act of getting out of bed felt like a victory? Where your to-do list seems endless, the phone won't stop ringing, your body is tired, and your mind won't shut off? That's what it feels like to be overwhelmed. But here's the truth: God never asked you to carry it all alone.

"Come unto me, all ye that labour and are heavy laden, and I will give you rest."
— *Matthew 11:28 (KJV)*

Being overwhelmed doesn't mean you're weak. It means you're human. And Jesus invites you to trade the pressure for peace. You weren't created to be everything for everyone. You were created to abide in the One who already is. Even when you feel like you're failing, God is holding you steady. Even when your emotions are high and energy is low, His strength is perfect in your weakness.

You don't have to keep pushing through in silence. God says, *"Bring it to Me."* And when you do, He gives you divine rest not just for your body, but for your soul.

Related Scriptures

- Matthew 11:28 – "Come unto me… and I will give you rest."
- Psalm 61:2 – "When my heart is overwhelmed: lead me to the rock that is higher than I."
- Isaiah 40:29 – "He gives strength to the weary…"
- Philippians 4:6–7 – "Be anxious for nothing… and the peace of God will guard your heart and mind."

Personal Reflection

I've had moments where I sat in my car in silence, just needing a minute to breathe. Moments when the world's expectations, my family's needs, and my own personal battles all felt like too much. And in those moments, I learned to say three life-changing words: "Lord, help me."

Not a long prayer. Not a fancy one. Just honest. And every single time, He showed up with peace, clarity, or just the strength to get through the next five minutes.

Prayer

God, I feel overwhelmed. I feel tired. I'm carrying more than I was built for. Today, I lay it at Your feet. Help me release the pressure, the guilt, and the fear. Replace it with Your rest, Your rhythm, and Your strength. In Jesus' name, Amen.

Faith Declaration

When I am overwhelmed, God is my anchor. I trade my heaviness for His rest. I do not walk alone I walk with the One who holds all things together.

Kingdom Key – Action of Faith

Take 15 minutes today to unplug. No phone, no noise, no multitasking. Go for a walk, sit in quiet worship, or breathe deeply and say: "God, I trust You to handle what I cannot. I surrender this moment to You."

Write a short list titled: "What I'm Releasing to God Today?"

Give each item to Him in prayer. You'll feel the weight lift as you exchange overwhelm for obedience and peace.

Journal Prompt

What's been weighing you down lately? What can you surrender today so you can make space for peace?

P – Peace

Stillness in the Storm
Stress, Sickness, Mental Turmoil, Uncertainty

Peace isn't the absence of chaos it's the presence of Christ in the middle of it. It's that supernatural calm when you should be panicking. That stillness in your spirit when your body is in pain. That unexplainable rest when everything around you is shifting.

"And the peace of God, which passeth all understanding,
shall keep your hearts and minds through Christ Jesus."
— *Philippians 4:7 (KJV)*

God never promised a life free from trouble. But He did promise peace in the trouble. Peace is a Person. His name is Jesus. And when you abide in Him, you don't have to wait for the storm to stop to feel safe. You can rest right in the middle of it, knowing He's in control.

The enemy will try to steal your peace with worry, diagnosis, fear, or confusion. But you have a choice: You can *guard your heart and mind* by trusting the One who holds your future.

Related Scriptures

- Philippians 4:6–7 – "Be careful for nothing… the peace of God shall keep your heart and mind."
- Isaiah 26:3 – "You will keep him in perfect peace whose mind is stayed on You."
- John 14:27 – "Peace I leave with you… let not your heart be troubled."
- Psalm 4:8 – "In peace I will lie down and sleep…"

Personal Reflection

There were nights I couldn't sleep facing treatment, financial pressure, unanswered questions. I'd lie awake trying to figure everything out. But peace came when I stopped trying to control it all and simply whispered, *"Jesus, I trust You."* His peace didn't remove every problem but it changed **me** in the middle of them. That's when I realized: peace doesn't come from understanding everything. It comes from trusting the One who does.

Prayer

Prince of Peace, calm the storm inside of me. Quiet the noise of fear, stress, and anxiety. I surrender my mind, my heart, and my body to You. Cover me with Your perfect peace and help me to rest in Your promises. In Jesus' name, Amen.

Faith Declaration

I am covered by the peace of God. I will not be shaken by what I see I will stand firm in who He is. His peace guards my heart and steadies my soul.

Kingdom Key – Action of Faith

Today, pause three times during your day. Each time, take a deep breath and say aloud: "Peace, be still." Speak it over your mind, your home, your emotions, or your body. Say it again and again if needed.

Then read John 14:27 out loud and declare: "I receive Your peace, Lord. I will not be afraid." Let peace lead you not pressure.

Journal Prompt

What situation is trying to steal your peace right now? How can you invite God's presence into it today?

Q – Quiet Trust

Faith Doesn't Always Shout Sometimes It Whispers
Singleness, Stillness, Waiting on God, Deep Faith

We often associate faith with action praying loudly, declaring boldly, or making bold moves. But there is another kind of faith that's just as powerful: quiet trust. It's the type of trust that waits without complaining, that hopes without needing an audience, that believes without having to prove anything.

"In quietness and in confidence shall be your strength."
— *Isaiah 30:15 (KJV)*

Quiet trust is when you stop striving and start resting. When you stop rehearsing the "what ifs" and surrender to God's "even if." It's when your soul says, *"I don't know how, but I trust that God does."* In seasons of singleness, uncertainty, or silence from heaven, quiet trust anchors you. It whispers:

- "He hasn't forgotten you."
- "He's still working."
- "You're still seen."

This kind of trust doesn't make a lot of noise. But it moves heaven.

Related Scriptures

- Isaiah 30:15 – "In quietness and in confidence shall be your strength."
- Psalm 62:5 – "My soul, wait silently for God alone…"
- Proverbs 3:5–6 – "Trust in the Lord with all your heart…"
- Lamentations 3:26 – "It is good that one should hope and wait quietly…"

Personal Reflection

There were times I wanted to *do something* to fix it. To rush the process. To make something happen. But God taught me that not every season is about *movement*. Some are about *trust.* Quiet trust isn't passive it's intentional. It's me saying, "God, I trust You more than I trust my timeline. More than my feelings. More than my fears." And that trust? It became my strength.

Prayer

Father, teach me how to rest in You. Quiet the noise around me and inside of me. Help me to stop striving and start trusting. Even when I don't see results, remind me that You are always working behind the scenes. I choose to trust You in stillness and surrender. In Jesus' name, Amen.

Faith Declaration

Even in silence, God is faithful. I don't need all the answers to trust His plan. My confidence is quiet, but it is fierce. I rest in Him.

Kingdom Key – Action of Faith

Find 10–15 minutes today to sit in complete stillness no background noise, no distractions. Just you and God. Say this simple prayer aloud:

"Lord, I trust You. I don't have to see it to believe it. I trust You because You are good."

Let that moment of stillness become your sanctuary. Let your silence be your strength.

Journal Prompt

Where are you tempted to rush God? What would it look like to practice quiet trust in that area instead?

R – Restoration

God Doesn't Just Heal He Restores
Loss, Marital Challenges, Broken Dreams, Renewal

Restoration is deeper than healing. Healing stops the bleeding but restoration gives you back what was stolen. It rebuilds what was broken. It breathes new life into what felt like ashes.

"And I will restore to you the years that the locust hath eaten…"
— *Joel 2:25 (KJV)*

God is not just the God of comfort. He's the God of comeback. What you thought was over He can reignite. What you thought was wasted He can redeem. Restoration isn't about returning to *what was* it's about being brought into something better. Maybe you've walked through divorce, lost someone you loved, been betrayed, or watched your dreams slip through your fingers. It may have left you feeling empty, tired, or forgotten.

But God promises to restore what life, people, or pain tried to take. He restores joy, hope, health, love, purpose and yes, even relationships.

Related Scriptures

- Joel 2:25 – "I will restore to you the years the locust hath eaten…"
- Psalm 23:3 – "He restoreth my soul…"
- Isaiah 61:7 – "For your shame ye shall have double…"
- Jeremiah 30:17 – "I will restore health unto thee…"

Personal Reflection

After seasons of deep loss and pain, I wondered if I'd ever feel whole again. I thought some pieces of me were just permanently gone too damaged to recover. But God reminded me that He doesn't just patch up the past He creates beauty out of it. Piece by piece, prayer by prayer, He started restoring my soul. Joy returned. Peace returned. Purpose returned. Not all at once, but faithfully, fully, and gently.

Prayer

Father, I give You every broken piece. The pain, the loss, the questions, the shame. You are the Restorer of my soul. Bring back what I thought I had lost my joy, my peace, my strength. I trust You to make all things new again. In Jesus' name, Amen.

Faith Declaration

God is restoring me. What I thought was lost, He is returning better than before. My story is not over it's being rewritten with redemption.

Kingdom Key – Action of Faith

Take a moment today to write a "Restoration List." List the things you've lost like time, confidence, relationships, opportunities and next to each one, write: "God is restoring this in His time and His way."

Pray over your list and declare Joel 2:25 aloud. Then say: "Lord, I receive Your restoration. Not partial, but full. I will be better, not bitter."

Journal Prompt

What areas of your life are in need of restoration? What have you given up hope on that God may still be working on?

S – Strength in Sorrow

God Gives You Power to Stand While You Heal
Grief, Pain, Cancer, Emotional Wounds

Sorrow has a weight all its own. It doesn't ask permission before it shows up. It hits hard, lingers long, and touches places you didn't even know could ache. But sorrow is not the end of your story.

"The Lord is my strength and my shield; my
heart trusted in him, and I am helped."
— *Psalm 28:7 (KJV)*

You can grieve and still have strength. You can weep and still be walking. Strength in sorrow doesn't mean you feel strong it means God is your strength when you don't. There are sorrows so deep they don't have words. The death of a loved one. The loss of a dream. The diagnosis that shifted everything. But God promises to be close to the brokenhearted and to carry you through the pain not rush you through it.

Sorrow may shape you, but it does not define you. The same God who wept at Lazarus' tomb is the God who lifts you from your own.

Related Scriptures

- Psalm 28:7 – "The Lord is my strength and my shield..."
- Psalm 34:18 – "The Lord is close to the brokenhearted..."
- Isaiah 53:3–4 – "A man of sorrows... surely He has borne our griefs..."
- Nehemiah 8:10 – "The joy of the Lord is your strength."

Personal Reflection

There were days when I smiled in public but broke down in private. Grief felt like a wave I couldn't escape. But even then, God was there sending strength through a friend's call, through a verse I needed, through just enough breath to get through the day.

That was strength in sorrow. It didn't always look like boldness. Sometimes it looked like *not quitting*.

Prayer

God, this sorrow is heavy. Some days I feel like I can't carry it. But You said You would carry me. So, I lean on You now. Be my strength. Be my comfort. Remind me that healing takes time and that You're with me for the whole journey. In Jesus' name, Amen.

Faith Declaration

God is my strength, even when I feel broken. He is walking me through sorrow and leading me into healing. My pain will not destroy me—it will develop me.

Kingdom Key – Action of Faith

Write a letter to your grief or pain. Be honest and say what you need to say. Then at the bottom, write: "I am not walking through this alone. God is my strength in sorrow."

Keep the letter in your Bible or prayer journal. It's not a goodbye to the pain but a declaration that *you're not bound to it anymore.*

Journal Prompt

What sorrow have you been carrying lately? How has God shown up in the middle of your pain?

T – Trust

Even When I Don't Understand, I Will Still Believe
Family, Uncertainty, Letting Go, Divine Timing

Trust is easy when everything makes sense. When prayers are answered quickly. When the path is clear and the provision flows. But real trust is forged in the fire when the "how" and "why" go unanswered, and you choose to believe anyway.

"Trust in the Lord with all thine heart; and lean
not unto thine own understanding."
— *Proverbs 3:5 (KJV)*

God never promised we'd always understand but He did promise that He would never leave us. Trust is not the absence of questions; it's the decision to place those questions in the hands of a faithful God. It's saying, *"I don't get it but I know You do."* It's looking at a child you raised who's gone astray… and trusting God with their return.

It's watching your plans fall apart… and believing He has better ones. It's standing at the edge of what looks like disappointment… and still stepping forward.

Related Scriptures

- Proverbs 3:5–6 – "Trust in the Lord with all thine heart…"
- Isaiah 55:8–9 – "My thoughts are not your thoughts…"
- Psalm 37:5 – "Commit thy way unto the Lord… trust also in him…"
- Romans 8:28 – "All things work together for good…"

Personal Reflection

I've had moments where I felt like I was falling no answers, no open doors, no rescue in sight. I had done everything I knew to do… and still, things didn't work the way I'd hoped. But it was in that surrender when I stopped striving and just trusted that peace came. And eventually, *so did breakthrough.* God didn't always explain but He always showed up.

Prayer

Lord, You see the things I don't understand. The prayers I've prayed that haven't been answered yet. The people I love that I can't fix. Teach me to trust You anyway. Help me to lean not on what I see, but on who You are. Strengthen my faith to believe again even without the full picture. In Jesus' name, Amen.

Faith Declaration

I trust God. Not because I understand everything, but because I believe in His goodness. He sees what I don't. His plan is perfect. And He is faithful to finish what He started.

Kingdom Key – Action of Faith

Take a piece of paper and write this sentence at the top: "God, I choose to trust You with…" Now list every person, problem, or situation you've been carrying on your own. When you're done, lift the paper toward heaven and say out loud: "I release this to You, Father. Not my will, but Yours be done."

Put the paper in your Bible as a reminder that *God is trustworthy even when life is uncertain.*

Journal Prompt

Where is God asking you to trust Him right now? What would change if you fully released control and believed His plan was better?

U – Unshakable Faith

I Will Not Be Moved
Health, Children, Delays, Opposition

Faith that lasts isn't built on ease or comfort. It's built in pressure, through storms, and in seasons where everything in you wants to quit but you stand anyway.

"Therefore, my beloved brethren, be ye steadfast, unmovable,
always abounding in the work of the Lord..."
— 1 Corinthians 15:58 (KJV)

Unshakable faith doesn't mean you never wobble it means you don't *fall.* It's the resolve to believe God's Word even when symptoms persist... when your child is still struggling... when the promise hasn't arrived yet.

Faith like this is not loud it's *rooted.* It's steady in prayer, consistent in worship, and anchored in who God is, not just in what He does.

There will be tests. There will be moments where it feels like everything is working against you. But if your faith is built on the Rock, *you will not be moved.*

Related Scriptures

- 1 Corinthians 15:58 – "Be ye steadfast, unmovable..."
- Psalm 16:8 – "I shall not be moved..."
- Hebrews 11:1 – "Now faith is the substance of things hoped for..."
- Isaiah 7:9 – "If you do not stand firm in your faith, you will not stand at all."

Personal Reflection

During treatment, I had days when I didn't feel strong. When I watched others get their breakthrough faster. When I wondered if my prayers were working. But I kept showing up. Kept speaking God's Word. Kept believing even with tears in my eyes. That's what unshakable faith looks like. Not perfect, but *planted.*

Prayer

Lord, plant me deep in Your Word. When winds blow and circumstances shake me, help me to stand strong in You. Let my faith outlast the storm. Help me trust You for myself, for my health, and for those I love. In Jesus' name, Amen.

Faith Declaration

My faith is rooted in Christ. I will not be shaken by what I see. I trust God's plan, His timing, and His power. I am unshakable in *Him.*

Kingdom Key – Action of Faith

Find a small rock and write the word "faith" on it with a marker. Place it somewhere visible a reminder that your foundation is solid. Every time doubt tries to creep in, touch that rock and declare: "My faith is built on the Rock. I will not be moved." You are not fragile you are *fortified.*

Journal Prompt

What has tested your faith the most? How has God helped you remain standing?

V – Victory

This Battle Is Already Won

Battles with Illness, Spiritual Warfare, Delays, Divine Triumph

Victory isn't a maybe it's a promise. As a child of God, you fight *from* victory, not *for* it. Even when the odds seem stacked, even when you're in the fight of your life God has already declared the outcome: you win.

"But thanks be to God, which giveth us the victory
through our Lord Jesus Christ."
— 1 Corinthians 15:57 (KJV)

Victory doesn't always look like immediate results. Sometimes, it's the ability to keep going. To stay in faith. To praise through pain. Victory is the mindset that says: *"This may be hard, but it won't be the end of me."* Whether you're battling sickness, fear, addiction, or the silent war in your mind know this: Jesus already overcame it. And because He won, you win too.

Related Scriptures

- 1 Corinthians 15:57 – "Thanks be to God, who gives us the victory…"
- Romans 8:37 – "In all these things we are more than conquerors…"
- Exodus 14:14 – "The Lord shall fight for you…"
- 1 John 5:4 – "This is the victory that overcometh the world, even our faith."

Personal Reflection

When I was facing one of the hardest seasons of my life physically weak, emotionally drained I would write down one word in my journal every day: Victory. I couldn't always see it. But I spoke it. Declared it. Believed it. And one day, I realized I wasn't waiting for victory anymore I was *living* in it. God had carried me through. And He's doing the same for you.

Prayer

Lord, thank You that I don't have to fight for victory I just have to stand in it. I receive the finished work of the cross over my life. Give me the strength to keep going, the boldness to declare Your promises, and the faith to see myself the way You do: victorious. In Jesus' name, Amen.

Faith Declaration

I am victorious in Christ. No matter how the fight looks, the outcome is already decided. I win. I overcome. I walk in power and purpose every single day.

Kingdom Key – Action of Faith

Write a declaration of victory and post it on your mirror, phone lock screen, or work desk. Say it aloud every morning this week: "I am victorious. This battle has already been won. I walk in power, healing, and favor because Jesus conquered it all."

Stand tall. Lift your head. You're not a victim you're a victor.

Journal Prompt

What battles have you been facing? How would your perspective shift if you believed that victory is already yours?

W – Warfare

Victory Begins in the Spirit
Spiritual Battles, Prayer, Authority, Persistence

Spiritual warfare is real. Your battle isn't just physical or emotional it's spiritual. The enemy doesn't just want your body tired or your heart broken he wants your *faith silenced.* But you've been given weapons. You are not powerless. In fact, you are dangerous to darkness when you stand in God's authority.

"For the weapons of our warfare are not carnal, but mighty through God to the pulling down of strong holds."
— 2 Corinthians 10:4 (KJV)

Every time you pray, you're waging war. Every time you speak the Word over your situation, you're tearing down lies. Every time you worship instead of worry, you're pushing back the enemy. Warfare doesn't mean you're weak. It means you're valuable. And if you're under attack, it's because you carry something *the enemy is afraid of.*

Don't be discouraged by the battle. Be reminded: you've already won.

Related Scriptures

- 2 Corinthians 10:4 – "The weapons of our warfare are… mighty through God…"
- Ephesians 6:12 – "We wrestle not against flesh and blood…"
- James 4:7 – "Resist the devil, and he will flee from you."
- Romans 8:31 – "If God be for us, who can be against us?"

Personal Reflection

There were nights I couldn't sleep heaviness hanging over me like a cloud. I didn't always know what to pray, but I knew Who to run to. And that's when I learned that *warfare isn't just about shouting it's about standing.* Standing in worship. Standing in truth. Standing in peace. Every time I didn't quit… I won another round.

Prayer

Lord, open my eyes to see the battle clearly and to fight wisely. Teach me to use the weapons You've given me. Strengthen me when I'm weary and remind me that You are with me in every fight. I take authority over fear, lies, and confusion. I choose victory today. In Jesus' name, Amen.

Faith Declaration

I am armed and dangerous. I don't fight for victory; I fight from it. No weapon formed against me shall prosper. God is fighting for me and through me.

Kingdom Key – Action of Faith

Today, read aloud Ephesians 6:10 –18 and spiritually put on your full armor. Then declare: "I am fully covered. I am fully armed. I am not afraid of this battle and I was born to win it."

If you've been quiet, today is the day to pray out loud. Take back the atmosphere of your home, your mind, and your emotions. Declare peace. Declare breakthrough. You are not on defense you are on assignment.

Journal Prompt

What battle are you currently facing? How can you begin to fight it differently spiritually, not emotionally?

X – Expectation

Hope That Refuses to Die
Faith for the Future, Patience, Hope in Delay, Believing Again

Expectation is the breeding ground for miracles. It's not passive hope it's *active belief* that God is not only able, but willing to move on your behalf.

"For surely there is an end; and thine expectation shall not be cut off."
— *Proverbs 23:18 (KJV)*

You may have waited a long time. You may have been disappointed before. But don't let that disappointment kill your expectation. Keep your eyes lifted. Keep your heart open. Keep your prayers flowing. Expect that God is working behind the scenes. Expect doors to open. Expect healing to manifest. Expect restoration to come. Expect joy to return. God responds to faith that leans in not faith that checks out.

So even if you've been in a holding pattern, don't stop expecting. Because delay is not denial and expectation keeps your heart in position to receive.

Related Scriptures

- Proverbs 23:18 – "Your expectation shall not be cut off."
- Romans 8:25 – "If we hope for what we do not yet have, we wait for it patiently."
- Psalm 5:3 – "In the morning I lay my requests before You and wait expectantly."
- Hebrews 11:6 – "Without faith it is impossible to please God…"

Personal Reflection

I've prayed prayers that didn't get answered the way I wanted or when I wanted. At times, I stopped expecting anything at all, thinking it would hurt less if I didn't hope. But God reminded me: *Faith without expectation is just survival. Expectation is trust in motion.*

So, I started praying with my eyes open again. Dreaming again. Believing again. And the more I expected, the more I saw.

Prayer

God, renew my expectation. Where hope has faded, breathe new life. Help me believe again dream again expect again. I trust that You are a good Father who delights in blessing His children. Stir up my faith to watch, wait, and walk in anticipation. In Jesus' name, Amen.

Faith Declaration

I live with holy expectation. I am not afraid to hope. What God has promised, He is faithful to perform. My expectation is alive, and my breakthrough is near.

Kingdom Key – Action of Faith

Today, write down three things you're expecting God to do in your life. Speak them out loud every morning this week. Say: "I expect healing. I expect provision. I expect God's best."

Then write a thank-you note to God as if He's already done it. Because in the spirit, *He has.*

Journal Prompt

What have you stopped expecting because of disappointment or delay? What would change if you believed God could still do it?

____

____

____

____

____

____

____

____

____

____

____

____

____

____

____

____

____

Y – Yielding

Letting Go So God Can Take Over
God's Will, Surrender, Trust, Obedience

Yielding is more than giving up it's giving *over*. It's saying, *"God, I choose Your will over my wants. Your timing over my control. Your way over my assumptions."* Yielding is where the real transformation begins.

"Not my will, but thine, be done."
— Luke 22:42 (KJV)

Jesus prayed those words in Gethsemane a place of deep pain and even deeper surrender. He didn't just yield out of obligation; He yielded out of trust. And His surrender led to salvation for the world.

In our lives, yielding might look like releasing the need to be right. Or giving up control in our family. Or trusting God with unanswered prayers.

It's not easy but it's powerful. Because every time you yield, you make room for God to move. You stop fighting battles that belong to Him. And you find peace in the place where you used to wrestle.

Related Scriptures

- Luke 22:42 – "Not my will, but thine, be done."
- Romans 12:1 – "Present your bodies a living sacrifice…"
- James 4:7 – "Submit yourselves therefore to God…"
- Proverbs 3:6 – "In all thy ways acknowledge Him, and He shall direct thy paths."

Personal Reflection

I've had times where I held on so tight to plans, to people, to outcomes I was sure were best. But the more I clung, the more frustrated I became. It wasn't until I said, *"Lord, I surrender"* that true peace arrived.

Yielding didn't change everything instantly but it changed *me.* And that was the breakthrough I didn't even know I needed.

Prayer

Father, I yield. I surrender my will, my plans, and my timeline to You. Teach me to rest in Your decisions, even when I don't understand them. Give me strength to let go and faith to trust that what You have is always better. In Jesus' name, Amen.

Faith Declaration

I yield to God's will. I let go of control and choose trust. I believe that what God wants for me is greater than what I want for myself.

Kingdom Key – Action of Faith

Take a blank page and write this across the top: "God, I yield these things to You…" List anything you've been carrying expectations, timelines, relationships, fears. Then lift the paper in your hands and say: "I place this in Your hands, God. I let go, so You can take over."

Keep this page in your Bible or prayer journal. Let it remind you: yielding is not weakness it's wisdom.

Journal Prompt

What is God asking you to surrender in this season? How would yielding bring you peace, even before you see results?

Z – Zion Mindset

Living with Eternity in View
Heaven, Purpose, Endurance, Eternal Reward

The word *Zion* represents the dwelling place of God, the heavenly Jerusalem. It symbolizes peace, victory, holiness, and eternity. When you live with a Zion mindset, you view everything on earth through the lens of heaven.

"For here we have no continuing city, but we seek one to come."
— *Hebrews 13:14 (KJV)*

This world is not your final home. Your struggles are real, but they are not permanent. Your body may break, but your spirit is eternal. Everything you've faced every valley; every victory is part of a greater glory being revealed. A Zion mindset is what allows you to keep pressing when life gets heavy. It's what reminds you that obedience matters, that suffering isn't wasted, and that God is preparing a place for you where there will be no more tears, no more pain, no more cancer, no more grief.

"They go from strength to strength, every one of
them in Zion appeareth before God."
— *Psalm 84:7 (KJV)*

Let that be your goal not just to survive, but to finish well. To live every day as one step closer to glory. To live with purpose, and to die in peace knowing you gave God your whole heart.

Related Scriptures

- Hebrews 13:14 – "We seek one to come…"
- Psalm 84:7 – "They go from strength to strength…"
- Revelation 21:4 – "God shall wipe away all tears from their eyes…"
- Philippians 3:20 – "Our citizenship is in heaven…"

Personal Reflection

Through all I've endured, one thing kept me anchored the promise of heaven. Knowing this world is not the end gave me strength in suffering and purpose in pain. It changed how I love, how I forgive, how I live. It reminded me that everything I do here echoes in eternity. And one day, I'll hear the words I long for most: *"Well done."*

Prayer

Father, thank You for preparing a place for me. Help me to live with heaven in mind. Let my focus be eternal, my love be bold, and my life bring You glory. Give me the strength to run my race well and to finish strong. In Jesus' name, Amen.

Faith Declaration

I am a citizen of heaven. My eyes are fixed on Zion. I live with purpose, I walk with power, and I press toward the eternal prize. I will finish well.

Kingdom Key – Action of Faith

Today, reflect on your legacy. Ask yourself:

- How am I preparing the next generation for Zion?
- What eternal impact am I making?
- What do I need to let go of so I can finish well?

Write a letter to your future self or to the next generation encouraging them to live with a Zion mindset. Speak from your healed, whole, and heavenly perspective. Seal it as a legacy offering of your faith.

Journal Prompt

What would change if you truly lived every day with heaven in mind? What do you feel called to do before you leave this earth?

Words of Encouragement

You made it through the valley. Through grief, pain, loneliness, sickness, and pressure. But more importantly you did not walk alone. God was there. Every letter. Every page. Every tear. And He still is. This is not just the end of a devotional it's the beginning of a renewed, unshakable, healed life. You've been anchored through it all. Now rise and walk in grace with a heart set on Zion.

About the Author

Melanie E. Lewis is a speaker, business strategist, and breast cancer survivor whose life was radically transformed through faith, pain, and purpose. As the founder of multiple businesses and initiatives, Melanie equips others to walk in financial freedom, legacy building, and spiritual healing while living authentically in their God-given identity. Through her transparent storytelling and unwavering belief in divine purpose, Melanie has inspired thousands to keep going, even when life hurts. Her voice resonates with women, survivors, and purpose-driven visionaries who are ready to rise again, trust again, and believe again. When Melanie isn't writing or speaking, she's empowering others through her publishing platform, A Believer's Story, where every day testimonies are turned into life-changing tools.

Booking & Contact Info

To book **Melanie E. Lewis** for your next:

- Women's conference
- Faith-based event
- Health and healing summit
- Business empowerment panel
- Podcast or media interview

Contact her directly or through her publishing team below:

Website: www.abelieversstory.live
Email: marketing@abelieversstory.live
Phone: +1 (313) 767-0521

A Believer's Story Publishing
Real Stories. Real Healing. Real Hope.

Made in the USA
Coppell, TX
15 October 2025